The Frog in the Pond

Written by Wil Mara
Illustrated by Cheryl Mendenhall

Children's Press®
A Division of Scholastic Inc.
New York • Toronto • London • Auckland • Sydney
Mexico City • New Delhi • Hong Kong
Danbury, Connecticut

For Matthew and Katelyn.
—W. P. M.

For Rachel, who likes frogs and bugs—even ugly ones
(but not to eat).
—C. M.

Reading Consultant

Cecilia Minden-Cupp, PhD
Former Director of the Language and Literacy Program
Harvard Graduate School of Education
Cambridge, Massachusetts

Cover design: The Design Lab
Interior design: Herman Adler

Library of Congress Cataloging-in-Publication Data

Mara, Wil.
The Frog in the pond / by Wil Mara; illustrated by Cheryl Mendenhall.
p. cm. — (A rookie reader: opposites)
ISBN-13: 978-0-531-17541-5 (lib. bdg.) 978-0-531-17775-4 (pbk.)
ISBN-10: 0-531-17541-3 (lib. bdg.) 0-531-17775-0 (pbk.)
1. English language—Synonyms and antonyms—Juvenile literature.
I. Mendenhall, Cheryl, ill. II. Title. III. Series.
PE1591.M37 2007
428.1—dc22 2006027344

1 2 3 4 5 6 7 8 9 10 R 16 15 14 13 12 11 10 09 08 07

I went outside yesterday.
I spotted a beautiful frog in
the pond behind my house!

It seemed like a very happy frog.

It sat on a log and croaked.

Suddenly, an ugly bug
crawled in front of the frog.

The frog leaned down and snapped it up!

I decided to keep the frog.
I took it off the log and brought it inside.

I put the frog in a tank with
a rock and some water.

I watched the frog all day and all night.

I gave the frog some more bugs to eat.

But the frog ate none of the bugs.
It even stopped croaking!

The frog seemed sad.

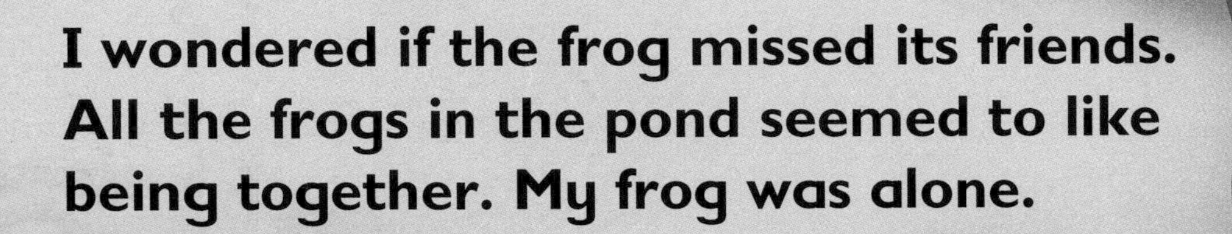

I wondered if the frog missed its friends. All the frogs in the pond seemed to like being together. My frog was alone.

Today, I brought the frog back to the pond and let it go.

The frog hopped on a log and started croaking. It even ate a bug that was crawling by.

The frog was happy again.
I was happy, too!

Word list (84 words)

(Words in **bold** are used as opposites.)

a
again
all
alone
an
and
ate
back
beautiful
behind
being
brought
bug
bugs
but
by
crawled
crawling
croaked
croaking
day
decided
down
eat
even
friends
frog
frogs
front
gave
go
happy
hopped
house
I
if
in
inside
it
its
keep
leaned
let
like
log
missed
more
my
night
none
of
off
on
outside
pond
put
rock
sad
sat
seemed
snapped
some
spotted
started
stopped
suddenly
tank
that
the
to
today
together
too
took
ugly
up
very
was
watched
water
went
with
wondered
yesterday

About the Author

Wil Mara has written more than seventy books, many of which are educational titles for young readers.

About the Illustrator

Cheryl Mendenhall studied illustration at Washington University in Saint Louis, Missouri, and at Art Center College of Design in Pasedena, California. She now lives and draws in Nashville, Tennessee, using everything from pencils and old toothbrushes to her computer.